The Book of Virtues

by the Students of
Tuckers Crossroads School
Lebanon, Tennessee

WRITE TOGETHER™ PUBLISHING
Nashville, Tennessee

Copyright © 2002 by
Tuckers Crossroads School
5905 Trousdale Ferry Pike
Lebanon, TN 37087
(615) 444-3956

All rights reserved.

Published by Write Together Publishing ™ LLC.
www.writetogether.com

ISBN 1-931718-37-7

Title: The Book of Virtues. Multiple authors.
Subject: Literary collections, poetry.

Project Coordinator: Lori Hassell

Cover Art: Sarah Alsup
                         Brittany Morrison
                         Christina Allen
                         Kasey Wright

For Write Together Publishing:

Publisher: Paul Clere
Editor-in-Chief: John D. Bauman
Book & Cover Design: Bill Perkins
Publishing Coordinator: Michael Pleasant

To publish a book for your school or non-profit organization that complements your academic goals or values, vision and mission, please contact:

Write Together ™ Publishing
533 Inwood Dr.
Nashville, TN 37211

phone: 615-781-1518
fax: 520-223-4850
www.writetogether.com

Table of Contents

Foreword State Representative Sam Stratton Bone xii
Introduction Lori Hassell xiii

The Virtue of Friendship
John Petty 1
Korin Dickson 2
Kelsey Stout 2
Tayler Moore 2
Sarah Fesler 2
Mary Beth Carney 2
John Snider..2
Ashley Cates 2
Adrian Jordan..3
Katie Dickson 3
Tabitha Sellars 3
Kendra Baine 3
Ashlee Cunningham..3
Stephen Williams 4
Eric Sorrels..4
Truman Tuck 4
Danielle Walling..4
Ashley Blowers 4
David Barrett 4
Ronessa Shannon 4
Leslie Reed 5
Allie Jordan..5
Dakota Hudson 6
Tyler Presley..6
Amber Rose 6
Jessica Wilson 6
Shannon Wall..6
Heather Fleming 6
Patrick Colley 7
Felicia Long 7
Alyssa Tippett..7
Halle Mathis..7
Brooke Lokey 7
Jade Hess 7
Adam Bowen 7
Kayla Carey 7
Andi Lyn Carney 7
Mallory Jennings 8
Kortnie Barrett..8
Natasha Hicks 9
Tatum Daily 10
Matthew Robinson 11
Samantha Holland 11
C.J. Wilson 12
Kaleena Coggins 13

Name	Page
Adam Stout	14
Carley Moore	14
Lauren Carr	14
Rachel Fesler	15
Samatha Hagar	15
Daniel Johnson	15
Jesse Watson	16
Cody Bryan	16
Michael Rosshirt	16
Justin Marek	17
Amber Hall	17
Samantha Potts	17
Rachel Snider	18
Katherine Watson	18
Emily Howard	18
Jenna Fithian	18
Harley Jones	18
Katie Reece	19
Amber Akin	19
Rebekkah Smith	19
Will Ferrell	19
Jessica Stephens	19
Jessica Warren	19
Lucas Oliver	20
Taylor Adams	20
Lacey Kendrick	20
Khalsie Barrett	20
Shaunte' Kvasnicka	20
Noelle Pritchard	20
Elijah Enoch	21
Jessica Counts	21
Heather Hamilton	21
Ashley Sisco	21
Hannah Neal	21
Tacy Ashworth	22
Kyle Bennett	22
Cassidy Carey	22
Paige Davis	22
Katlin Eakes	22
Samantha Finley	22
Jacob Ford	22
Chance Hudson	22
Justin Johnson	22
Danielle Jones	22
Hunter Jordan	22
Shaquille Moore	23
Emily Prindiville	23
Kristal Shackelton	23
Allie Stanley	23
Zach Ward	23
Hunter Warren	23
Rob Warren	23
Hunter Jordan	23

Justin Johnson 23
Danielle Jones 23
Alex Dowell 24
Zach Gardner 24
Alicia Heady 24
Jonathan N. Pena 24
Ashton Kemerling 24
Joshua Rittenberry 24
Elizabeth Pritchard 24
Jonathan Reed Grandstaff 24
Kyleigh Presley 24
Jonathan David Walling 24
Mackenzie Stuck 24
Blake Smith 24
Ciarra Ribbons 25
Breanna Hunter 25
Ashton Kemerling 25
Drew Bridges 25
Brittany Collins 25
Victoria Frick 25
Olivia Jennings 25
Hannah Wright 25
Blaze Wilmeth 25
Jacob McDonald 25
Victoria Murphy 26
Colin Pritchard 26

The Virtue of Perseverance

Clay Turnbull 27
Taylor Dill 27
Karmen Dickson 27
Ashley Sisco 28
Jessica Bailey 28
Ryan Hackett 28
Christina Allen 29
Branson Hammrich 30
Shane Mattingly 30
Ashley Lindsey 30
Sara Stout 31
Frances Christina Nesbit 31
William Mofield 32
Ashley Ashcraft 32
Shane Greer 34
Johnathan Howard 34
Brian Lindsey 34
Vincent Syler 35
Tara Chambers 35
Josh Barnett 35
Kayla Baird 36
David Apple 36
Brian Wright 36

The Virtue of Courage

Andrew Gammon 37
Jessica Johnson 37
Chase Hudson 37
Rachel McCaleb 37
Martin Mobley 38
Aaron Geiger 38
Marequis Dobson 38
Shelby Gardner 38
Jessica Bailey 39
Kaleb Hacket 39
Reed Sorrels 39
John-Michael Cook 39
Eric Sorrels 39
Savannah Taylor 39
Kalee Kendrick 39
Philip Diehl 40
Canaan Neal 40
Mamie Hassell 40
Tanner Dedmon 40
Sarah McDonald 40
Adam Powell 40
Anna Demumbra 40
Jameson Sorrels 41
Hunter Welch 41
John Daniel Mobley 41
Caroline Cavender 41
Abra Snider 41
Patrick Hall 42
Anthony Giles 42
Katelyn Spencer 42
Christopher Gray 43
Adam Stanley 43
Andrew King 44
Chelsea Ashcraft 44
Shelby Isbell 44
Mallory Jennings 44
Jacob Hearn 44
Ashley Reed 45
Kayla Carter 45
Marcus Springer 45
Kenneth Shrum 45
Sarah Cates 46
Sara Satterfield 46
Jacob Wilson 46
Daniel Raines 46
Susan Madderon 46
Autumn White 46
Jonathon Raines 46
Keith Hightower 46
Michele Miller 47
Derrick Babbitt 47
Jake Smith 47

The Virtue of Faith

Kelsey Hackett 49
Tyler Baird 50
Jacob Garland 50
Layce Booker 50
Jacob Hearn 50
Megan Adams 51
Kristen Smith 51
Mary Beth Johnson 51
Jake Smith 51
Tyler Baird 52
Shay Coggins 52
Karmen Dickson 52
Kayla Carter 52
Jessica Davis 52
Samantha Baxter 52

The Virtue of Generosity

Nicole Norman 53
Jason Sells 53
Eric Neal 53

The Virtue of Honesty

Hunter Hudson 55
Dew Wilmeth 55
Hailey Speck 55
Sarah Dillard 55
Coty Oldham 55
Merritt Powell 56
Dyllan Holby 56
Justin Bridges 56
Amber Jacobs 56
Kyle Craighead 56
Shelby Harper 56
Mollie Prindiville 57
Bradley Morris 57
Ashley Reed 57
Brandon Chambers 57
Kayla Bush 57
Abigail Garland 57
Landon Marek 57
Billy Barr 57
Tazz White 58
Jeremy Sevier 58
Thomas Howard 58
Sarah Cooper 59
Lauren McCarty 59
Devin Loftis 59
Hardie Sorrels 60
Dillon Bane 60
Drew Hulse 60
Jimmy Bowers 60
Logan Bryan 60

Mark Sandoval 60
Greg Hulse 60
Philip King 61
Christina Anderson 61
Allison Dowell 61
Monya Nikahd 61
Shelby Gullion 61
John Shelton 61

The Virtue of Responsibility
Ryan Hackett 63
Conner Garcia 63
Josh Garcia 63
Russell Lewis 64
Brock Fanchier 65
Matthew Barker 65
Austin Hackett 65
Taia Ashworth 65
Joy Lewis 65
Latasha Davis 66
Ian Isbell 66
Johnathan Dodd 66
Andy Stamps 66
Austin Bryan 66
Jameson Sorrels 66
Drake Barr 66
J. T. Streng 66
Brandi Shrum 66
Andy Stamps 67
Emily Brown 67
Logan Watson 67
Blake Carter 67
Kyle Bruce 67
Cole Condra 67
Ashley Buck 67
Chris Rodgers 67
Rachel Sandoval 68
Kasey Wright 68
Cynthia Frick 68
Paige Robinson 68
Broderick Enoch 68
Alex Babbitt 68
Taylor Walker 68
Michael Dobson 68
Kristin Cook 68
Daniel Stewart 69
Kaleb Woodcock 69
Shrader Doray 69
Ashley Baynes 69
Madeline Jennings 69
Kaleb Woodcock 69
Rebecca Fiehweg 69
Justice McFall 70

  Becky Cox 70
  Allison Jones 70
  Megan Dowell 70
  Taylor Ford...70
  Amber Cooper 71
  Kristen Dillon...71
  Bobby Fraley..71
  Kyle Fleming 71
  Zane Horstmeyer 71
  Hailey Justice 71
  Buddy Rollins 71
  Chase Goolsby 71

The Virtue of Compassion
  Ashley Lyles 72
  Ana Gregory..72
  A.J. Snider 73
  Brittney Goode 73
  Seth Barber 74
  Kathye Stone 74

The Virtue of Loyalty
  Jack Whetnall 75
  Hunter Hudson 76
  Devin Jones...76
  Chelsea Odom 76
  Josh Bryan 76
  LaJerrica Cowan 76
  Tabitha Dailey 76
  Will Hightower 77
  Calvin Starks 77
  Jennifer Hollis...78
  Maggie Thompson 78
  Amber Carney 78
  Asia Clark...79
  Chad Fisher 79
  Jeremy Officer 79
  Brittany Pickler...80
  Lorie Diane Marsh..80
  Rebekah Marie Wolfenbarger 80
  Ashley Cook 81
  Shara Garcia 82
  J.J. Fannin...82
  Amber Mizelle 83
  Patrick Hall...83
  Tara McClenon 84
  Kristina Johnson...86
  Lorenzo Sawyers 86
  Kimberly Bendt 86
  Brittany Morrison...87
  Tom Cruz..87
  Shada Carter 88

Leah Morgan 88
Dana Sorrells 88
Sarah Alsup 88
Shawna Shrum 89
Crystal Tucker 89

The Virtue of Work
Garrett Fanchier..91
Andrica Leach 91
Joseph Wilson 91
Casey Boyd...92
Jessica Etheridge...92
Terrence Coggins 92
Josh Dickson 93
Brian Sevier 93

STATE OF TENNESSEE
HOUSE OF REPRESENTATIVES

Sam Stratton Bone, Jr. • State Representative • 46th District
Trousdale and Wilson Counties

Secretary, Agriculture Committee • **Member,** Transportation Committee

The basic roots of virtue begin with the family. Once virtue has been instilled in a child, it can be enhanced by educational experiences. A well-rounded education includes academic, emotional, physical and creative development. Once mastered, these skills enable our children to become successful adults.

Although teachers can encourage, parents can mentor, and friends can influence, the creativity of a child's mind takes flight on its own wings. The ability to express oneself and affect the lives of others with virtuous words and actions is a priceless ability.

This collaboration of stories and poetry has encouraged children to embrace their creativity. While we as parents and educators are responsible for guiding our children, I believe that there are many things that we can learn from them. It is my hope that we will all be inspired by the expressions of goodness and virtue contained within this book.

Sam Stratton Bone, Jr.
State Representative
House District 46

TUCKERS CROSSROADS SCHOOL
5905 TROUSDALE FERRY PIKE
LEBANON, TENNESSEE 37087
Lori Hassell, Principal
Linda Bruce, Assistant Principal
(615) 444-3956
FAX: (615) 444-3958

It is with great pride that we present *The Book of Virtues*, the first published book of our students' writing. The Tuckers Crossroads Family appreciates your support of this project.

As reflected in our mission statement, The Promise of a Future: Knowledge~Character~Inspiration, we believe strongly in the training of the heart and mind toward the good. The national tragedy of September 11, 2001, has brought to life the importance of these virtues which include friendship, compassion, loyalty and work. As you read our students' original works, I believe you'll be touched by their insight and genuine desire to be citizens with hearts where virtues dwell. I thank each student who contributed and each teacher who encouraged them.

I would also like to thank Mrs. Whirley, Mrs. Rittenberry, Mrs. Blevins and Mrs. Presley for coordinating this project and Mr. Stratton Bone, our State Representative, for his comments.

Sincerely,

Lori Hassell

Lori Hassell
Principal
Tuckers Crossroads School

The Virtue of **Friendship**

Friends
Remember forever
Imagination
Eternity
Never end
Dignity
Special
Honesty
Important
Play together
John Petty, Grade 6

Illustration by Kristen Smith

If you ask me what friendship is, I would say that it is about kindness and caring for others. If people make fun of your friend, you should stand up for them, but don't hurt them.
Korin Dickson, Grade 5

I believe in friendship because it is the key to our earth. If we all don't have friendship, what's going to happen? I just think we should have friendship because it is a very good thing and it's the link to a very big heart!
Kelsey Stout, Grade 4

I believe in friendship because friendship is the relationship you have with your friend, a special bond between you and your friends. Friendship means you will always be loyal and trustworthy to your friends.
Tayler Moore, Grade 4

I believe in friendship because if someone did not have a friend, what would you do? Everybody has to have a friend. Without a friend, you wouldn't have any fun.
Sarah Fesler, Grade 4

I believe in friendship because my friend tells me everything. Her name is Ashlee. She is nice. I believe in her because she has known me since first grade. I still believe in her.
Mary Beth Carney, Grade 4

I believe in friendship because I believe in my friends and they believe in me. That's what makes friendship.
John Snider, Grade 4

I believe in friendship because I have a bunch of friends. If I did not have friends I probably would not believe in friendship. I think everyone has a friendship with someone.
Ashley Cates, Grade 4

I believe in friendship because it means respecting your friend and helping out your friend when they need help. It also means being kind to your friend and treating them the way you want to be treated. Friendship is always being a friend no matter what.
Adrian Jordan, Grade 4

I believe in friendship because you should play with everybody. You should be friends with everybody and go to everybody's birthday party. You should have fun with everybody. Even though they were not your friends before, you still should be friends with them. If I did not have friends, I would not believe in friendship. Always be friends with everybody.
Katie Dickson, Grade 4

I believe in friendship because you can have more friends. Friendship is also being nice and stuff like that. Once one of my friends came over and asked if I wanted to play, so I did. One of your friends may do that.
Tabitha Sellars, Grade 4

I believe in friendship because if people did not, then we probably wouldn't like each other and would not want to talk to anyone anymore. We would not have a friend to tell stuff to and could not play together.
Kendra Baine, Grade 4

I believe in friendship because having a friend means showing you care for them and seeing how they show care for you. I also believe in friendship because when someone's down and feeling blue and they need a friend or two, I will be right by them to comfort them at anytime they need it.
Ashlee Cunningham, Grade 4

I believe in friendship because when someone is new to a school, most people are shy. You should ask them to be your friend. Friendship means you should be their friend.
Stephen Williams, Grade 4

Friendship means being kind.
Friends stay with you through thick and thin.
Friends always tell the truth.
Friends never let you down.
Friends that make promises never break them.
Eric Sorrels, Grade 3

A friend is a person that you can trust.
A friend makes a promise and does not break it.
A friend cheers you up when you are sad.
A friend is nice.
Friendtastic!
Truman Tuck and Danielle Walling, Grade 3

A good friend plays with you when you are very lonely. A good friend is nice to you. A good friend doesn't let you down. If a good friend hits you, they will say they're sorry to you. A good friend will not be bossy to you. A good friend won't tell a secret to anyone.
Ashley Blowers, Grade 3

I can play with my friend. You can play on the monkey bars.
David Barrett, Grade 2

Friendship is a good thing to have. I like to let people borrow my stuff, and I make sure they won't lose it. I let people borrow my eraser, my pencil, my glue, my crayons and my scissors.
Ronessa Shannon, Grade 2

A friend tells the truth. A friend does not ever let you down. Friends help you when you are hurt. A friend is there for you. Friends never lie. A friend is someone that does not hit or kick you. A friend is someone caring. Friends always show respect to you. A friend is someone that is nice to you who you are there for.
Leslie Reed and Allie Jordan, Grade 3

Illustration by Rachel Sandoval

Friends should not hit or kick each other. They should help each other if they fall. Also, if you ask them to keep a secret, they should keep it. I have a lot of friends. We sometimes fuss, but we are still friends. I care about my friends when they get hurt. If you want a friend, ask someone to be your friend.
Dakota Hudson, Grade 3

A friend is a person who doesn't let you down.
A friend is a person who is caring.
A friend is a person who is always there for you.
A friend is a person who is always sharing.
Tyler Presley, Grade 3

I have been nice to my friends and my friends have been nice to me. I love you, friends.
Amber Rose, Grade 2

I think that friendship is good because I think that you should help your friend. We can help each other because helping is good at school.
Jessica Wilson, Grade 2

If somebody lost something, you should help them find it. If your friend got hurt, help them. Help somebody with things.
Shannon Wall, Grade 2

I think that friendship is helping people. If I am going to check the mail and see my friend fall on her bike, I will go help her get up and then take her home.
Heather Fleming, Grade 2

Friendship means being best friends, not hitting or being mean to people, and not calling them names.
Patrick Colley, Grade 1

A friend is a person that you can count on and that you can trust.
Felicia Long, Grade 1

A friend is nice to me and helps me, like Sarah and Taia.
Alyssa Tippett, Grade 1

Friendship means that someone plays with you. They are nice and happy.
Halle Mathis, Grade 1

Friendship is being nice to your friends and never being a big bully.
Brooke Lokey, Grade 1

Being kind to others is friendship. Good friends play nice together.
Jade Hess, Grade 1

Being nice to your friends is what friendship means.
Adam Bowen, Grade 1

Being nice to everybody and not calling anyone names is friendship.
Kayla Carey, Grade 1

Treating my friends nice and not ever being mean to them is friendship.
Andi Lyn Carney, Grade 1

One morning Janie was woken up by the ring of a telephone. She answered it and it was her best friend Rachel. She said, "You are late again for school." Janie looked at her alarm clock. Her brother, Scott, had unplugged it again. Sometimes she hated him. He was only eight and was a pain. She told Rachel that she would be late for her history test review and notes for tomorrow. Rachel said not to worry. She said she would take care of it for her.

Janie got dressed and did her hair in a messy ponytail as usual. Her mother had her cereal ready downstairs at the table. She rushed through with only one bit of Lucky Charms and a sip of orange juice. When she got to the bus stop, of course, the bus had already come and gone. So she ran as fast as she could and got there just in time for math. She saw Rachel at her locker with a piece of paper in her hand. She asked, "What is that?" Rachel said, "It is the history notes I made for you." "Thanks, Rachel, you are a real friend. Come on, we are gonna be late for math."

After school, Rachel had saved Janie a seat on the bus. She told her to come to her house that night and they would eat butter popcorn and study their history notes. When she got home, she told her mom that she was going to Rachel's at 5:00 p.m. She went to her room to call Rachel and talk. Scott, her brother, had put honey on the phone! She was about ready to kill him when she realized it was 4:30 p.m. and she needed to be going. So she got ready and went to Rachel's. Rachel already had the table ready with notes and popcorn. When they finished, she thought she understood it all. The next day on her test, because of Rachel's thoughtfulness, Janie made an A!

Mallory Jennings, Grade 5

Friendship is something nice,
Ten times better than sugar and spice.
A friendship is when you share,
Also when you really care.
Sometimes you start feeling funny,
Or even jumpy,
But most of the time you feel like you should.
That feeling is good.

Kortnie Barrett, Grade 6

I never had a best friend.
I always wanted a friend who had time to spend.
I always wanted a friend who's nice
And a friend who always thinks twice.

I always ask people to be my friend.
They never think I have time to spend.
I hope I'll have a friend at the end of the year
And grow up to have a nice career.

We have a new student who's a girl.
Her name's Baryl.
She's really nice
And she always thinks twice.

My best friend accepts me for who I am.
I went over to her house to see her lamb.
I spend all my time with her
And it just occurred to me,
That's she's my friend.

I tried my hardest for a friend.
We both think we have time to spend.
She likes all kinds of people
Who are being themselves.

You never give up.
You'll have some luck.
So find a friend
To lend you a hand.
Natasha Hicks, Grade 7

There once was a man named Mr. Custard. Mr. Custard was an average man who had two twin daughters, two twin sons and a wife. Mr. Custard had something that no one else in the neighborhood had—he had the meanest neighbor, Mr. Augolo. Mr. Augolo was a mad doctor who made potions that could turn people into animals. What kind of animals, you ask? Snakes, fleas, birds, alligators, monkeys, rats, apes, hawks, wolves, deer, antelope, lions, whales, and even ants. Every potion that the doctor made had succeeded.

There was a seven-year-old boy who had a very strange name, Shateri. Shateri had a bunch of friends in the neighborhood. They would play ball and kick the kickball into Mr. Augolo's yard. The very next morning, Mr. Augolo decided that there was only one way to stop the kids from kicking the ball into the yard, and that was to threaten them. They next day when the boys were playing, by accident the ball flew into Mr. Augolo's yard. He was waiting for them. He picked up the ball, and sure enough Shateri was the one to come after it. Shateri asked, "May I please have my ball back?" Dr. Augolo said, "If I ever see this ball in my yard again, I am going to turn your friends into animals!" Shateri took off with the ball to tell his friends about what had just happened to him.

Mr. Custard's daughter heard Mr. Augolo say that to Shateri, and she told her dad. He said, " What!" Next he marched straight over to the doctor's house, and the doctor answered the door. Mr. Custard said, "Have you ever thought of being nice?" The doctor replied by saying, "No, but could you teach me? The only reason that I'm mean is because I have a boring life." Mr. Custard said, "Sure I can under one condition: if you promise to tell everyone that you are very sorry." "Okay", said the doctor.

Three months later, Shateri and his friends kicked the ball into the doctor's yard again. This time the doctor was waiting with the ball. He said to Shateri, "Can you forgive me, and can we be friends?" Shateri said, "I have two words for you, yes, and yes!"
Tatum Daily, Grade 6

Friendship is the most wonderful thing in the world. I am going to talk about what makes a really good friend. For me honesty, compassion and generosity are the most important virtues of true friendship.

Honesty is the most important part in a friendship. To tell a lie or the truth is the best test of friendship. I know friends lie. Everybody does once in a while, even me. Honesty gives you more friendships because people trust you more because they know they can depend on you.

Compassion is the second thing needed to be a good friend. When someone special dies in your family and you are very sad, your friends feel sad for you, too. They try to make you feel good by doing fun things with you. You feel compassion from friends when they make you feel better.

Generosity is the third thing needed to be a good friend. When you need help with anything, friends will help you as much as they can. If you need help on your homework and your friend helps, that is generosity. It gives you a sense of caring and giving.

I have learned to be a better friend by these virtues, and you should too. Remember, a true friendship is made of honesty, compassion and generosity.
Matthew Robinson, Grade 6

Pinch of trustworthiness
4 phone calls a week
3 cups of kindness
5 letters a month
5 Saturdays of shopping
1 cup of honesty
1 teaspoon of love
4 study days together
2 cups of faith

Mix gently and softly. To have the right touch, take turns stirring. Fill with hugs. Sprinkle with joy and laughter. Cover with bright smiles. Bake till golden-yellow. This makes a very good heap of friendship. Serves 2
Samantha Holland, Grade 7

Friendship is really important to somebody with or without friends.

On the way to school one Monday morning, I saw my friend hanging out with a group of kids, even though normally she always comes and waits for me at my house and we walk to school together. Thinking she must have forgotten to come by and wait for me, I walked up to her. She looked at me and walked away. In shock, I stopped then watched her laugh with a conceited bunch of girls that I despise.

Through the miserable day, I sat despondently. After eating the despicable, phony, school cafeteria lunch, I heard there was a rumor going around, started by one of the girls, that my friend was hanging out with now, saying that I said something terrible about her! I don't understand why Cori would believe such a destructive thing like that when we have been friends for so long.

She was still ignoring me days later, and I was friendless and lonely. Since she was the only person I used to talk to all the time, I had no one else on earth I could talk to. I saw her having the most fun with the girls from planet "Stuck Up." She knew I was lonely.

A couple more days passed. Tired of the silence, I walked up to Cori and held her arm so she couldn't go away. I said, "Cori, why would you believe a detestable rumor that you heard from someone you know that you can't trust?" She exclaimed, "I don't know, I should've asked for details. I'm sorry." I forgave her and we swore we would talk it over before blaming anyone so we can be friends forever.

C.J. Wilson, Grade 6

There are several ways to make friendships. Making friends takes hard work, and keeping them takes a lot of compassion, loyalty, and honesty on a mutual basis.

The value that is going to be mentioned first is compassion. Friends need to be compassionate to each other because we all need someone to lean on when we're down. Compassion is the bridge to friendship because you have to feel for your friends. If a friend is sad or feeling in doubt, you have to help them and let them cry on your shoulder.

Loyalty is the next building bridge to friendship. In friendship you need loyalty because it's what allows your friends to count on you.

When a friend is not loyal, then that friend can't be counted on. Loyalty is also needed in friendship because if you can't count on your friends, who are you going to count on?

The last and final value that is being mentioned is honesty. You have to be honest because you can lose many friends when they find out you lied. Telling the truth to a friend isn't always an easy thing to do, but it's the right thing to do to make your friendship stronger. Sometimes not telling the truth will nag at you until you tell the friend the truth.

There are several values I know of that make friendships stronger. Being compassionate, being loyal, and being honest are the values that I share within my friendships.

Kaleena Coggins, Grade 8

Illustration by Abra Snider

It was a beautiful fall day. Birds were chirping and squirrels were running around. It seemed like a day when nothing could go wrong. But it was a day of sorrow for some families. Tuckers Crossroads School was having a day of prayer. It was the day James B. Wilson was lowered into the ground. When you hear that name, it kind of makes you stop and think about the boy that had brought happiness to many. It was like yesterday when we got the last look at my friend. James was a kid who was energetic, but one day he changed our lives. James's friends and family will never forget him. Jesse Watson was his best friend. Those guys had a good friendship. It's now dark in some of our lives without him. We're still waiting for someone else to light up our lives again. But my friend is gone.
Adam Stout, Grade 7

Together forever we'll always be.
For years and years that was our creed.
Then one day I moved away,
Hoping friends we'd always stay.
Even now as years go by,
I often think of you and cry.

Our love is strong, our friendship great,
Yet is it enough to take on fate?
Over the years you'll stay in my heart.
Your memory too strong to ever part.

As days go by and I don't hear,
I start to think that you don't care.
Even when you stop thinking of me,
Your best friend I'll always be.
Carley Moore, Grade 8

Friendship
Like a bracelet
Memories linked in line
Forever buried in our hearts
Priceless
Lauren Carr, Grade 7

What would you do if you had no friends?
What would you do if you felt your life was coming to an end?
What would you do if your only friend were to die?
What would you do if all you could do was cry?

If you don't know, I'll tell you. You'll keep going on until the very end, stopping for nothing, nothing at all.
Rachel Fesler, Grade 8

1 cup honesty
2 cups trustworthiness
3 cups patience
1 tablespoon of perseverance
1 teaspoon loyalty
1/3 cup faith
4 cups compassion

Stir well for several years. See if your friendship has gotten stronger. If you have all of this in a friendship, you should have a wonderful friendship.
Samatha Hagar, Grade 8

A good friend is someone who's caring and nice.
A good friend is someone whose friendship is without price.
A good friend comes with you through thick and thin.
A good friend likes to grin.
A good friend is someone trustworthy.
A good friend is worth having.
A good friend is someone who is there all the time.
A good friend likes to spend time with you.
A good friend is someone who will stand tall.
A good friend is someone who won't act like they know it all.
Daniel Johnson, Grade 8

Today was different; all the dark, gloomy clouds are out. It seems like just yesterday the sun was out. It seems like just yesterday that there were no dark, gloomy clouds. It seems like just yesterday that we were playing war in your yard. It just seems like just yesterday that we were racing bikes down your driveway. It seems like just yesterday that we were playing video games, laughing, and talking on the phone.

But today, today was different, because you weren't there. Then another friend helped me through this hard time. They said no matter what they would always be there. I think a good friend will help you and be with you no matter what happens.

That is what I think makes a good friend.
Jesse Watson, Grade 8

I should have been there,
It would have not been the same.
You'll never know how much I care.
Life just seemed like a great big game.
Now that you're gone, I feel like I've lost.
The world seems empty without you, your life was the ultimate cost.
It seemed that there was nothing you could not do,
You'll never know how much I cared about you.
I thought we'd be together until the end.
I thought we'd stick together like glue.
You would never give in.
James, I should have been there.
Cody Bryan, Grade 8

Friendship
Loyal, honest
Playing, joking, trusting
School, work, church, town
Enduring, forgiving, giving
Caring, reliable
Daniel
Michael Rosshirt, Grade 8

Friendship
Easy, good
Helping, sharing, cooperating
Affection, devotion, playmate, buddy
Collaborating, working, assisting
Gentle, simple
Brotherhood
Justin Marek, Grade 8

If you see someone lost in a world of confusion,
And you know they're on their own,
Walk right up and hold their hand,
And tell them they're not alone.
That's a friend!

If you love someone more than anything,
But they're not of any relation,
Don't you care what anyone says
Because they are all you can think of.
That's a friend!

If you see someone who is down and out,
And you don't know what to do,
Just walk right up and give them a hug,
And tell them, "I love you."
That's a friend!

If you know that your friend will have to leave,
And that they will soon depart,
Take your time to be with them,
Until you know you have touched their heart.
That's a friend!
Amber Hall, Grade 7

Love means that you love someone very much. I love my mommy, daddy, my baby sister and everyone in my family.
Samantha Potts, Kindergarten

1 cup love
3 teaspoons long talks
A pinch of spice
1 cup fun
2 pints care
A lot of time

Set out for 30 minutes and eat with friends.
Rachel Snider, Grade 6

Friendly
Relationship
Inspiring
Energetic
Nice
Daring
Sharing
Hilarious
Interested
Peace
Katherine Watson, Grade 6

    Friendship makes me feel like I'm honest and trustworthy. Friends help me when I need help so I will help them when they need help. I know if I am sad I can just call them and they always make me feel better. It's really good to have friends that you can talk to.
Emily Howard, Grade 4

    To me friendship is a way to have fun, whether it's talking or playing outside. Friendship is an important thing to me. I think it's important to have someone to count on, play with, or just talk to. I think friendship is a great thing to have.
Jenna Fithian, Grade 4

    I will share with my friend if I have a new toy. I will share and share.
Harley Jones, Grade 2

Friendship means to be nice and kind to each other. Let's say somebody lost a paper and found it, then turned it in to the teacher. This is an act of kindness from a friend. To have friendship means to stay together even when you are mad or happy.
Katie Reece and Amber Akin, Grade 4

I think friendship is about sharing my toys and about giving someone something like a ball or a necklace or a ring. I think that friendship is about playing with everyone and being nice to one another.
Rebekkah Smith, Grade 2

Friendship is having a good friend that helps someone get up on the monkey bars and pushes them in a swing and plays with them and takes them home, takes them to a bike ride in Nashville and takes them on a boat and takes them to the zoo, a swim with the dolphins and scuba diving in the pond. A friend also takes them to a yard sell and gets a stereo and some matchbox cars and a pair of shoes and goes to Wal-Mart and gets a pack of shoestrings and socks and when we got home we play on the computer.
Will Ferrell, Grade 2

I think friendship is something that you can do every day. I love having friends. Do you like having friends?
Jessica Stephens, Grade 2

I think friendship is helping someone that needs a friend. I think friendship is helping a good friend that is hurt. I will walk him or her to the teacher. I think friendship means being nice to one another. I think friendship means having a good friend. What do you know about friendship?
Jessica Warren, Grade 2

I think friendship is about sharing a toy and being nice to one another. Being a friend is being nice to one person.
Lucas Oliver, Grade 2

I think that friendship is about helping people do their work and getting to go outside.
Taylor Adams, Grade 2

I think friendship is about helping one another. I think friendship is about sharing. I think friendship is about playing with each other. I think friendship is about sharing with somebody.
Lacey Kendrick, Grade 2

Friendship is where you are a friendly person that is a nice person. And I am nice.
Khalsie Barrett, Grade 2

I think friendship is to help a friend if they are hurt by telling the teacher. If she is crying, I will help her and will walk her to the teacher.
Shaunte' Kvasnicka, Grade 2

I think friendship is being kind and caring for each other. Friendship is looking out for each other. Love and never give up on friendship.
Noelle Pritchard, Grade 2

I think friendship is being someone's friend and sharing with them. I think responsibility is picking up after yourself and being on time at school and bringing books back to the library on time.
Elijah Enoch, Grade 2

I think friendship is not yelling out when somebody is talking and treating everybody the way you want to be treated and being nice. If somebody drops something, pick it up and make a friend.
Jessica Counts, Grade 2

Friendship is good when you have a friend. I have one and her name is Hailey Speck. I like her. I have a dad who is cool. He works on tractors at a co-op and I come to school and have fun. My mom wears my coat at home.
Heather Hamilton, Grade 2

Two people caring,
Two people who give each other a helping hand,
Two people who keep secrets,
Two people helping each other through problems,
Two people who don't talk bad toward others,
Two people who are together through all eternity,
A friendship like this should be cherished.
Ashley Sisco, Grade 8

Many people have a good friendship with somebody. Friendship is very wonderful to people. I have a lot of friends. Friendship is where you have a best friend, and you respect them and treat them the way they want to be treated.
Hannah Neal, Grade 5

What Is a Friend?
Mrs. Grant's Kindergarten Class

You play together and be friends.
Tacy Ashworth, Age 5

It means be nice and play with others. Give food to people and kids toys.
Kyle Bennett, Age 5

To be nice and friendly.
Cassidy Carey, Age 5

Play and be nice to each other and not be mean to each other. If they swing, don't push them out of the swing.
Paige Davis, Age 5

Being nice and helping others. If someone fell I would help them up.
Katlin Eakes, Age 5

Don't treat others mean. Friends help others.
Samantha Finley, Age 5

To be nice and to share toys.
Jacob Ford, Age 5

Friends play together and do things together and play on the ship together.
Chance Hudson, Age 5

To be nice to others and not hurt them.
Justin Johnson, Age 5

Share and play together. Share the computers.
Danielle Jones, Age 5

Share toys and bicycle. Be nice.
Hunter Jordan, Age 5

School. Play ball. Barney.
Shaquille Moore, Age 6

They play with you all the time. When you see them they give you a big, big hug.
Emily Prindiville, Age 5

You share your bikes with them. We share our toys. My friends like to play with me. We like to play cars.
Kristal Shackelton, Age 5

Be nice. Share. Playing with each other.
Allie Stanley, Age 5

It means to help and share.
Zach Ward, Age 5

You play with each other. We like each other. We play with each other all the time.
Hunter Warren, Age 5

Take turns and share. You should care about others.
Rob Warren, Age 5

Share your toys and be nice. Share your bike. Care about your friends!
Hunter Jordan, Age 6

To play with others and to share.
Justin Johnson, Age 5

To be nice and to share. Be nice to each other and play together.
Danielle Jones, Age 5

Friendship Is...
Mrs. Judy Nosal's Kindergarten Class

To be a friend, you ride bikes.
Alex Dowell, Age 6

To be a friend, you have to play with others.
Zach Gardner, Age 5

Friendship means to play and share.
Alicia Heady, Age 5

To be a friend, be nice, play cars, trucks, and you can share glue.
Jonathan N. Pena, Age 5

Friends just play.
Ashton Kemerling, Age 5

To be a friend, play with others and let them come to your party.
Joshua Rittenberry, Age 5

Friendship means you play and need to share.
Elizabeth Pritchard, Age 5

Friendship means you are good to everybody. You go to movies a lot.
Jonathan Reed Grandstaff, Age 5

Friendship means you aren't mean. You are nice.
Kyleigh Presley, Age 5

Friendship means you don't want to fuss or fight.
Jonathan David Walling, Age 5

Friendship means coloring with your friends.
Mackenzie Stuck, Age 5

A friend is kind to others and plays with others.
Blake Smith, Age 5

A friend is playing with somebody. My cousin is my friend.
Ciarra Ribbons, Age 5

My cousin is my friend and always plays with me. His name is Christopher and we play outside and inside together.
Breanna Hunter, Age 5

Friendship is play. Friends write together and color, and cut, and glue.
Ashton Kemerling, Age 5

Friendship Means…
Mrs. Lisa Stanley's Kindergarten Class

Friendship means being nice and playing with friends.
Drew Bridges, Age 5

Friendship means being nice.
Brittany Collins, Age 5

Friendship means sharing stuff.
Victoria Frick, Age 5

Friendship means getting to do stuff, like play.
Olivia Jennings, Age 5

Friendship means playing.
Hannah Wright, Age 5

Friendship means playing and having fun.
Blaze Wilmeth, Age 5

Friendship means being good and playing with others.
Jacob McDonald, Age 5

Friendship means that you should be nice to your friends and others because you should be nice to everyone, not just one person.
Victoria Murphy, Grade 4

      Fun
       Trustworthy
  Laughing
     Ni**c**e
    Fun**n**y
      Re**s**pect
       Happy
    Play**i**ng
     Res**p**onsible
Colin Pritchard, Grade 5

The Virtue of **Perseverance**

Positive you can do something to reach your task.
Every time you don't give up leads to perseverance.
Ready to never give up.
Somebody that helps others has faith in their abilities.
Everything you do to reach your goal is perseverance.
Victory is what you feel when you reach your goal.
Each person at school is being responsible when they help someone.
Responsibility leads to a finished task.
Achievement leads to perseverance.
Never give up.
Can do it! Can do it! Can do it!
Effort will help you reach your goal.
Clay Turnbull, Grade 6

Perseverance
Stay with it
Never lose hope
Perseverance
Taylor Dill, Grade 5

Perseverance
Never quitting
Always doing
Perseverance
Karmen Dickson, Grade 5

There once was a girl who was named Morgan. Morgan was only 13 years old. She had always dreamed of being a reading teacher. Morgan wasn't rich and she wasn't poor, but she could always use someone's help. Morgan went to high school. She didn't like it. Morgan wanted to quit but her mother said, "Look how you are getting closer to your dream." Morgan thought about it so she decided to stay in school. Morgan had made excellent grades in reading and as well in other subjects. When the school asked Morgan what she wanted to be, she said, "A reading teacher."

Several years later, Morgan graduated from high school. After everyone graduated, they said they had one student who wanted her dreams to come true. They asked Morgan to come back on the stage. Morgan smiled real big. The principal was on the stage and handed Morgan a scholarship to go to college. After that night of graduation, Morgan went home, packed some clothes and some other stuff, and went to college. After she graduated from college, Morgan returned to her hometown. Morgan had become the best reading teacher around. Morgan always said you should never give up on your dreams.
Ashley Sisco, Grade 8

Perseverance
Learning to stick with it
Always jumping over obstacles
Peseverance
Jessica Bailey, Grade 5

,

Perseverance
Stick with
What you do
And don't give up
In what you
Are doing.
Ryan Hackett, Grade 5

Illustration by Dana Sorrells

There is this teacher at my school that I look up to. She is a big role model for me. She has all the virtues in one. She's a friend when you need one and is compassionate and kind. She's loyal and patient and works hard at being a good teacher. As a teacher, she puts faith in her students and believes they can do whatever they put their minds to. She even lifts you up when you're down. Above all those virtues, there is one that shows more than all the rest, and that is her perseverance.

This teacher has a disease that affects her muscles. Every day it's as if nothing is wrong, but I know in my heart that she has to keep reminding herself to just keep going on.

One day, close to the beginning of the year, she sat down to give us a spelling test. When we were through, she went to get up, but she couldn't straighten up. She scared all of us because you could see she was in pain, but she just put her books down and tried again. Even though we had to help her anyway, just her not giving up was awesome. She then told us what she had, but not to feel sorry for her, that she was fine. She even apologized for spilling her water. I love her very much and thank her for being such a great role model and light to me. When I feel like I can't go on, all I have to do is think of her and I'll gain my perseverance.

I love you, Mrs. Blevins!

Christina Allen, Grade 8

You have perseverance
When you never give up.
If you have perseverance,
You will really get pumped up.
My dad has perseverance.
He will always try his best
And yet never had to rest.
He always has fun
And never has to run.
And most of all he will never let you down
Because he never stands around.
Branson Hammrich, Grade 6

    Perseverance means to never give up. I know some people with perseverance. First of all, there is my dad. For instance, when I first started baseball, I stunk, and who was there keeping me on my toes? If it weren't for dad, I wouldn't be the good baseball player that I am. So if you read this story, take my advice and always have perseverance. You'll feel real nice.
Shane Mattingly, Grade 6

    When you try and jump one hundred ropes, at first it seems you've lost all hope; but when you get to fifty, it seems very nifty. That's what perseverance means.
    Perseverance, what are you? You are something I can do, something I keep my mind to. So now let's find out what you do.
    Perseverance, what do you do? What you do is so evident, because you keep me confident. So now you know what you do.
    Now we can think you through. So let's review. Perseverance is keeping to a task. It's when you don't ask. So now that we are through and we've done our review, let's put it all together.
    We are putting it together, so let's think about the task. Keep my mind on something, and confidence will be jumping.
    Perseverance, perseverance, perseverance.
Ashley Lindsey, Grade 6

Prepared to tackle your tasks.
Everyone can have perseverance.
Responsibility leads to a finished promise.
Special qualities for everyone.
Even you can make a change.
Responsibility also leads to faith.
Always have faith in yourself and in other people.
Never give up on anyone.
Constantly have more faith in yourself.
Effort to have more faith.
Sara Stout, Grade 6

Being the King,
Being the almighty,
Being the perfect person,
Being in such excruciating pain,
Being the one who has to endure people's sin,
Being the one that loves everyone no matter what.

If I were the one who had taken in all these responsibilities,
I would have given up long ago.
But you keep pressing on and on,
Ready for the next obstacle.
Frances Christina Nesbit, Grade 8

I once had friend. He was the best that you could have. He was loyal, honest, and showed great compassion. He was always there for me. On November 4, 2000, my best friend was taken away from me. It took me a while for it to sink in. The next day, I could not go to school. I talked to myself. I had to show perseverance. I had to fight through. I went to the funeral home that day. That's when I realized my friend had been taken away. I thought to myself, I should have been there. I could have stopped my friend from this horrible fate. I went to his casket and saw him dead. He wore a Red Wings cap on the top of his head. The next day I felt a sorrow come over my head. I burst into tears as I saw his desk. I still can't imagine why he had to die. My friend is gone and he's not coming back this time.

In Loving Memory of James Wilson
1988 – 2000

William Mofield, Grade 8

When I stepped in the door of my new parents' house, I knew this was going to be a big adventure for me! I only had two things on my mind – my new family and my locket. I was just really scared about my new family, I felt I might not be good enough for them. Before I moved here, I was not in the high class. I was poor. I guess they just picked me up off the streets. My locket has to do with my real parents. They were real young whenever they had me and left me on the street when I was two. A cop saw me, picked me up and took me to the orphanage. I was there for 13 years. Now I am 15, and I am finally out of there.

My locket is just not a normal locket. It is half of a locket. My parents gave it to me when I was born. I think my parents had the other half with my picture in it. My mom's name was Terrlin and my dad's name was Rusty. My mom has long, red hair and a round face with green eyes. My dad has short, blonde hair. He is skinny with a narrow face and blue eyes.

My name is John Michale. I look mostly like my dad. I have blonde hair and china blue eyes. I am very skinny. I really don't know if I had any brothers or sisters. Whenever I look down at my lovely locket, it reminds me of them.

My new parents' names are Judie and Scot. Judie has long, dark brown hair. She is on the skinny side. Scot has light brown hair with hazel eyes. My new mom and dad's house is huge, the biggest house I have ever seen in my life. I live upstairs in a medium size room. The walls are blue, the carpet is white. There is a big, big bed and beside that is a nightstand. Judie and Scot came to the door and said, "Make yourself at home. If you need any help, just tell us." They went back downstairs. I started to put my stuff away when Judie yelled, "John Michale, get washed up for dinner." After I did, I went down to eat supper.

When I got down there, we ate supper. Judie and Scot said, "So, John Michale, what do you know about your parents?" "Well, I don't know much about them, but I do know I am going to find them." Judie and Scot just smiled.

The next day, John Michale began his search. He made copies of their pictures and hung them around town. The posters said, "If you have seen these people, please call 555-7255." After days and months, no response. John Michale went up to his new parents and said, "I am not trying to say I don't love you. You all have been great to me. But something is just telling me to go out there and find them." Judie and Scot said, "If I was a kid that did not know my parents, I would do that too."

I was still on the search. It had been one year and three months. I was not going to give up. The next day there was a call from a person named Terrlin and she asked for me. I picked up and said, "Hello." Terrlin said, "John Michale, is that you?" I said, "Yes this is John Michale." Terrlin said, "Do you know who this is?" I said, "No." She said, "This is your mom." I said, "Is it really?" She said, "Yep." I said, "When can I see you?" She said, "How about tomorrow at your new house and I will bring your dad." When they came up to the door, the first thing I saw was the locket, and I knew it was them.

We talked and talked.

This is my story of my perseverance. From that moment we always stayed in touch

Ashley Ashcraft, Grade 7

In the small town of Zanesville lived a boy that always tried his hardest in school and at home. When his parents got divorced, his grades went slowly down hill. He didn't know who was going to take him to school, or anyplace for that matter. He kept trying but he didn't understand what it meant to be divorced. He tried even harder than before. His mom and dad tried to comfort him during the difficult time, but that didn't help. He went to his friends, but they didn't care. It wasn't their problem. He went to the counselor at school. She helped some by telling him that, if he kept trying, he would make it just fine. He took her advice and he was back. He became a straight-A student on the principal's list. He still remembers that year when his mom and dad got divorced, but he persevered.
Shane Greer, Grade 7

I'm usually afraid to go out at night.
I always get a little fright.
I'm telling the truth when I say I'm afraid of the dark.
I don't know why, sometimes I just stay inside.

I keep trying to find ways to get over my fears.
I will sometimes play at night, but I just feel the fear.
But when a friend is over,
My fear is over.

And when they're gone,
My fear is back once again.
So I realized, my friends help me
Because when they're here, my fear isn't.
Johnathan Howard, Grade 7

In the virtuous world of virtues, there are several virtues to know. With my trustworthy advice, you'll understand the three keys to perseverance. The three most important keys are starting something, not giving up, and finishing.

First off is starting something. Once you start something, you shouldn't stop. The reason you don't stop is because it will be harder to start again. You also get it done faster and can do more stuff you like after you're finished.

Next, the most important thing is not giving up. If you give up, the job may never get finished. It's kind of like homework—you don't want to do it, but you do it anyway so you'll get finished. So even if you do stop for water, start back up again.

Last, but certainly not least, is finishing. Once you finish, you can then move on to something that you enjoy instead of working. When you finish, you should feel a great deal of confidence. Finishing should also leave you feeling a great deal of pride.

So take my advice. Use the virtue of perseverance and follow the three simple keys: starting, not giving up and finishing. I hope you use them wisely.
Brian Lindsey, Grade 7

Ah! Perseverance, my dear friend in hand, never shall be banned. For as long as I live, I shall sing a song of its reverence to all people and shall never bind you to the clever tricks of truant fugitives who use deception to lure you to lies.

You should rise up and tell them that they are demented tempters, sent to demolish all good, and that you will not become deceived or indebted to them at any time or place. In this way, you will persevere until the end, will sincerely stand against oppressors, and will not bend the other way.
Vincent Syler, Grade 7

I have lots of perseverance. In all of my classes I have perseverance. I would like to have straight A's or A's and B's, but I don't. I have a learning disability, so it is kind of hard for me to make good grades, but I have perseverance.
Tara Chambers, Grade 8

Perseverance is to strive to believe in what you want to. Dream as big as you want to. Dream of red, white and blue. Everybody has a chance to strive. We will all stay alive. We will survive because we were born in America.
Josh Barnett, Grade 8

I love a really good friend that has perseverance. She tries and tries at what she is trying to accomplish until she accomplishes it. Her name is Brittany Pickler. She is a true and loving friend. Nothing could break our friendship. Brittany was having trouble in social studies and her grades were not up to par. Brittany loves sports, but the rule was that you had to have grades above a C. Brittany was playing volleyball at the time, and it was time for the coach to check grades. When the coach looked at Brittany's grades and told her she was out until her grades were up, she was very depressed. But she wasn't going to give up, she knew she could bring up that grade, and that is what I like about her. For the next week, Brittany turned in all her work and studied for every test. When she looked at her grades again, she was so happy because the grades were now up to par; therefore, she got to play volleyball again. Brittany tries hard at everything she does, and I will try my best to be just like Brittany because I like her for who she is and the way she does things.
Kayla Baird, Grade 8

When I think of perseverance, I think of the policemen and firemen who struggle to find life in the rubble of the twin Trade Towers. While using bare flesh, they lift the wreckage. As one man lifts, the other looks for a spark of life and that chance to save a human being. As they look for days that turn into weeks that turn into months, the chance of finding life grows dim. That is what I think of when someone says perseverance.
David Apple, Grade 8

Perseverance is a good quality that we need to see more of these days. If you have a dream, go for it. If you don't get it the first time, don't give up. I know I wouldn't. I know some people who strive to achieve their goals at the utmost expense. These people are the humans who work their hardest and strive to surpass their rivals.
Brian Wright, Grade 8

The Virtue of **Courage**

Courage is…

Confidence
Overcoming
Unafraid
Resolving
Achieving
Grit
Endurance
Andrew Gammon, Grade 6

When I think of courage, I think of Leslie. She was very brave to cross the creek. She was very fearless. Leslie was ready to do everything no matter how scared Jess was.
Jessica Johnson, Grade 5

Courage means to be fearless.
The fireman has a lot of courage because he went into a burning house and saved a little baby. If the mom had been scared, the baby would have died.
Chase Hudson, Grade 5

Courage reminds me of a person who is brave, fearless, heroic, and has a lot of grit. Some of the characters in *Bridge to Terabithia* demonstrate courage like Leslie and Jess.
Rachel McCaleb, Grade 5

Once upon a time, Tim was walking down a street. Then he saw a house on fire. He heard someone scream, so he ran in and he looked and looked. Then he saw a small girl sitting in a chair, but he couldn't get to her because of the burning hot flames. He finally made up his mind to run through the flames and get the girl. He ran back through the flames. When the firefighters got there, Tim had severe second-degree burns. Luckily, the little girl was fine. When Tim recovered, he was awarded the Badge of Courage.
Martin Mobley, Grade 5

If you have experienced courage, you know that great feeling. The feeling of courage is so wonderful; it's simply amazing. At this time I will tell you what courage means, how you acquire it, and when it should be used.

What does courage mean? It does not mean to have bravery for just one minute. It means to stand up and stay there until the very end. An example is to stand up to a bully in order to protect a friend.

How do you acquire courage? You acquire it from friends. You need to have friends, family, or even a stranger nearby to get courage. I, for one, usually don't get courage, but when I do get courage, I stand to the very end.

When should you use courage? I think that any time someone is in trouble is the right time. I had an incident like that happen to me once. My friend was getting bullied, and I stood up for him.

To feel courage is to feel great. I know that is what courage means. How to acquire it and when it should be used are all up to you to decide.
Aaron Geiger, Grade 6

When I think of courage, I think of Leslie, a character of Terabithia. Leslie is fearless and likes to help other people even if they have been mean to her in the past.
Marequis Dobson, Grade 5

I was scared when I wanted to go back into a backbend, but now I know how to do it and I'm not scared.
Shelby Gardner, Grade 2

Learning to be brave
Always facing my fears
Courage
Jessica Bailey, Grade 5

Firemen are brave. They go and fight the flames that start. Firemen choose to risk their lives for others to save the lives of millions. Firemen have lots of courage.
Kaleb Hacket, Grade 3

Courage means that you stay calm when something bad is happening. Courageous people are never afraid. Courageous people are always brave. Courageous people are always there when you need them.

Courageous people believe in helping others. Courageous people don't let us down. Courageous people try to keep us safe. Courageous people do not have any fear. Courageous people help us when things go wrong.
Reed Sorrels, John-Michael Cook and Eric Sorrels, Grade 3

Courage is not being a super hero. Courage is doing something good.

Courage is standing up to a fear you've had a long time. Courage is not giving up and doing something you have been afraid to do for a long time.
Savannah Taylor, Grade 3

Courage means not being scared or frightened. Courage means being able to do something some people would never want to try.

Courage means being worthy to try new things. Courage means being encouraged to do something that you may not achieve the first time.

Courage means being strong and believing in yourself.
Kalee Kendrick, Grade 3

One day there was a boy who was afraid of spiders. His friend had a spider collection. He was afraid to go in his friend's room. But one day he had the courage to stand up to his fears of spiders and went into his friend's room. There he saw the spider collection. He reached in and picked up a spider—he wasn't scared. He got over his fear of spiders.
Philip Diehl, Grade 3

Courage is not being scared like when I was little. My mom takes me to the beach, and now I am not afraid of the water.
Canaan Neal, Grade 1

Courage is not being afraid. I like to play with my cat, but I am afraid of dogs.
Mamie Hassell, Grade 1

Courage is being brave and not being scared. A fireman would be brave to go into house to save someone.
Tanner Dedmon, Grade 1

Courage is not to be afraid. I am scared of the dark and don't like to stay by myself.
Sarah McDonald, Grade 1

Courage is not being scared. I'm not afraid to jump off of the high dive.
Adam Powell, Grade 1

When you have courage that means you're brave and you're not afraid of things.
Anna Demumbra, Grade 1

Courage must be like the people who were on the plane that crashed into the big building. They must have been brave.
Jameson Sorrels, Grade 1

Courage is when you're brave like when the dog was after me. I got away on my four-wheeler.
Hunter Welch, Grade 1

When you go to bed and it's dark outside, you need to be brave. That's courage. Courage is being brave when you do new things.
John Daniel Mobley, Grade 1

Courage means to be brave. If a big bully says mean stuff to you, don't get scared.
Caroline Cavender, Grade 1

The courage of the families,
Who need God to help them out.
We need to drop down on our knees,
He will help us in our doubt.
We must be united together,
To work for the better,
And courage will help us out.

When we don't know what to do,
Turn to God who is true.
The courage is strong
And will help us along.
In God we must trust
To get us out of the dust,
And courage will help us out.
Abra Snider, Grade 8

Courage is leaving your friends behind,
while you travel to the frontlines,
where memories will only comfort you.

Courage is fighting along a stranger,
and standing in the face of danger,
and deep inside you know the end is near.

Courage is standing amidst your foe,
and your secrets you'll never let go,
no matter your suffering.

Courage is hoping again to see,
the home of the brave and the land of the free,
while captures show no pity on your life.

Courage is returning home,
after being alone,
for so long.

People call you hero,
because of you they'll forever strive,
knowing that courage kept you alive.
Patrick Hall, Grade 8

Firemen
Are there
On the bad days.
They do anything helpful
To save a lot of lives
And fight to put out the blaze.
Anthony Giles, Grade 7

    Courage is the ability to conquer fear or despair. Courage is a very strong word. To have courage, there are three main things you have to do: you have to be brave, be truthful, and not be shy.
    Being brave is something a lot of people don't do. If you want to be brave, stand up for what you believe in or what you think is right.

Also be, daring, not the daring that gets you in trouble, but the daring that comes from doing what's right.

Being truthful has a lot to do with friends within themselves. Don't lie to other people or to yourself. Also, be respectful to others. Do for them as they would do for you.

If you are shy, you might not have much courage. The reason is because you would be too shy to stand up and say what you believe in. You shouldn't avoid anything you want to get involved in either. And make sure you're not bashful.

Courage is a wonderful thing to have. Don't let anything small get in your way of having courage.
Katelyn Spencer, Grade 7

Courage is a rare and wonderful treasure,
A special trait we cannot measure.
No matter how large the task,
Fearless ones bear their souls without being asked.

Courage comes in packages big and small,
Putting one thing first—liberty for all.
Spirit and bravery are the main concern,
Asking for nothing in return.
Christopher Gray, Grade 7

I watched number 32 going up and down on the basketball court. I see him make all the points, but I sit here on the bench waiting for my turn. I listen to the ball that goes boom, boom, boom. Now it is my turn, but I have to go up against this really big guy. We are down by one, ten seconds to go, my teammate passes the ball to me, but the big guy is blocking me. I know, though, that God will give me the courage. I let the ball go, and we score and win! Nevertheless, after the game the ball will go boom, boom, boom.
Adam Stanley, Grade 6

3 cups of bravery
1 tablespoon of encouragement
a dash of fear
2 tablespoons of prayer
1 cup of humility
1 tablespoon of faith
2 cups of strength
Andrew King, Grade 6

Courage
Being brave
Facing your actions
Courage
Chelsea Ashcraft, Grade 5

Courage
Be brave
Can you be brave
Use it in every way
Brave
Shelby Isbell, Grade 5

Courage is a strong feeling. You have to be able to stand up for yourself and be strong. Be tough and, whatever goes wrong, have courage and go for your goal.
Mallory Jennings, Grade 5

Courage is when you are brave. Courage makes you a better person. Courage makes you feel confident. Everybody should have courage.
Jacob Hearn, Grade 5

Courage
Being brave
Standing up to fears
Courage
Ashley Reed, Grade 5

To have courage, you must be brave. To have courage, nothing can stand in your way. To have courage, you need it in sickness. To have courage, there's nothing to hide. To have courage, you know what to do.
Kayla Carter, Grade 5

Courage
Is to finish
What you start.
Marcus Springer, Grade 5

Courage means to stand up for your family. We think you should say "No" to drugs and smoking. It takes more courage not to fight, but to respect the other person.
Kenneth Shrum, Grade 4

We think courage is important because some people are brave, strong, healthy, and honest. If someone is harming you, speak up and tell him or her to stop. We will have the courage to stand up and say "No" to drugs. By saying "No" to drugs, you will be healthy. Courage is being honest and standing up for a belief. When you have courage to stand up for yourself, then you will be strong!
Sarah Cates and Sara Satterfield, Grade 4

One day we went home after school and turned on the TV. For some reason it was on Channel 2. We were watching the news and then we saw a SPECIAL REPORT. It said a plane hit a building. Firemen, policemen and road workers were working everywhere. We then discussed how courageous and brave these working people were to endanger their lives for others.
Jacob Wilson and Daniel Raines, Grade 4

We believe in courage because we know the United States will win the battle against terrorists. The courage and self-confidence of our president, who is meeting danger without fear, will lead us through this time of fear. The brave soldiers will have courage to go to war if needed. God Bless America!
Susan Madderon and Autumn White, Grade 4

Courage means to be brave and strong, like if you were going to pick up a log and didn't have the courage to do it, but then you got the courage. Or like if you were going go into the woods but you were scared to, but then you got the courage to do it.
Jonathon Raines, Grade 2

I hope the rescue workers have the courage to help people from the plane crash in the hospitals in New York.
Keith Hightower, Grade 2

Courage
Proud, sensation
Brave, fearless, courageous
Like a great soldier
Brave
Michele Miller, Grade 5

Courage is when you do something very frightful. Courage is when you wake up at night and hear sounds and go back to sleep. Soldiers have courage when they go to war. That is what courage is.
Derrick Babbitt, Grade 5

One day there was a mouse. His name was Courage. He did not like his father. Also he was bigger than him. One day he went to his older brother's house, who told him to get out of this house. But he did not go anywhere. So one day he went back to his brother's house. His brother opened the door and said, "I told you to go and never come back."

His little brother said, "You didn't tell me to never come back."

"Yes I did," he said. "Well, okay, I didn't" his older brother finally said.

"I just wanted to talk to you about dad. I wanted to know how you made it through with father mouse around."

"I had to do a lot of chores and not talk back to father mouse."

So the little mouse went home and finally had the courage to do all the chores for father.
Jake Smith, Grade 5

The Virtue of **Faith**

F is for firm belief
A is for allegiance
I is for imagination
T is for truth
H is for honesty

As all of them mean Faith.
That is what I think faith is.
Kelsey Hackett, Grade 6

Illustration by Ashley Jacobs

To the people in New York on September 11, 2001, it was a normal day. In a matter of minutes, their lives were taken away. Many families lost their loved ones and never knew their lives would be taken away. Terrorist attacks across our country caused things to change in our country. We are Americans and we stand together for the love of our freedom.
Tyler Baird, Grade 5

Roses are red.
Violets are blue.
Sugar is sweet.
I have a lot of faith in you.
Jacob Garland, Grade 5

If you have faith in God,
You have everything you need.
If you have faith in your family,
You have trust.
If you have faith in yourself,
You will be confident.
If you have faith in your friends,
You will grow strong.
If you have all these things,
Then you have love in your heart.
You will grow up to be a wonderful person.
Layce Booker, Grade 6

I think faith means believing what you believe in, being a religious person, and being trustful.
Jacob Hearn, Grade 5

F is for finding who you are.
A is for achieving who you are.
I is for identifying what your values are.
T is for truth which lies in you.
H is for holding the faith in you.

F is for fairness which lies in you.
A is for achieving what you have to do.
I is for identifying what your values can be.
T is for truth which lies in me.
H is for holding the faith for all to see.
Megan Adams, Grade 8

Faith is something that should stick to you just like glue.

Faith is something you have to have through both the good times and the bad.

Faith will get you through the day even if things don't go your way.

If everybody in the world had faith, the world would be a better place.
Kristen Smith, Grade 8

When I think about faith, I think about people that trust their family, best friends and more. Faith is about trusting people that you know you can trust.

Faith is like someone that is brave, someone you can trust that is like your best buddy.
Mary Beth Johnson, Grade 5

Faith reminds me of when May Belle, a character in *Bridge to Terabithia*, followed Jess to his secret hideout. Jess had to trust her to not tell where the hideout was.
Jake Smith, Grade 5

I think faith means to trust someone and be hopeful, to believe in each other, and to be fair and be caring.
Tyler Baird, Grade 5

Faith is about trusting someone, someone who you can trust. I am faithful because my friends trust me.
Shay Coggins, Grade 5

Everybody has faith down inside. Here's a story about a girl that didn't think she had faith.

There was this horrible tragedy that happened in New York. Terrorists hijacked four planes, and a little girl's mom died. She was extremely upset. I told her she had to believe in herself. Several weeks later, she came up to me and said my words really helped.
Karmen Dickson, Grade 5

Faith is something that you have. You don't need someone to give it to you, it's already there. Faith can be a name, but most of all it's something inside. Sometimes faith can let you down, but it can also bring you back up. You can have faith in God and in others too. But most of all faith is in you!
Kayla Carter, Grade 5

Faith
All caring
I believe
Truth is an important virtue
Hopeful
Jessica Davis and Samantha Baxter, Grade 4

The Virtue of **Generosity**

Giving
Extra-abundant
Noble
Equalized sympathizer
Rhapsody for hospitality
Overflowing acts of tenderness
Sharing exquisite thoughts of great minds
Impromptu thoughts of forgiveness
Tainted in unselfishness
Yearning every day to always be a Good Samaritan.
Nicole Norman, Grade 8

Generosity
Thoughtful, unselfish
Sharing, giving, providing
Policemen, firefighters, nurses, doctors
Dying, loving, fulfilling
Plentiful, faithful
America
Jason Sells, Grade 8

1 cup Kindness
2 cups Giving
1 teaspoon Loving
1 cup Patience
3 teaspoons Happiness
1 tablespoon of Smiles
a dash of Friendliness
1 cup Helpfulness
1 cup Nobleness

All together they make up the recipe for generosity.
Eric Neal, Grade 6

The Virtue of **Honesty**

Honest
Outstanding
No lying
Everyone tells the truth
So people can believe you
Truth
You do not lie
Hunter Hudson, Grade 3

I think honesty is a good thing. Cleaning your room is a good thing.
Dew Wilmeth, Grade 2

I think honesty is taking care of your things and not lying. If your friend tells you to do something, you should do it. That is what I think.
Hailey Speck, Grade 2

I think honesty is when your friend lets you borrow something, and you lost it, and you do not say, "My mom made me throw it away." I also think that honesty means that if you say, "I am going outside," and you wake your baby up from his nap, you would get in trouble.
Sarah Dillard, Grade 2

I believe in honesty because it is the right thing to do. If someone gets blamed for something and you did it, you need to admit that you did it.
Coty Oldham, Grade 4

I believe in honesty because it is the right thing to do. Honesty is like finding something that is not yours then giving it back to the person who it belongs to, even if you really want it.
Merritt Powell, Grade 4

I believe in honesty because it's telling the truth and being loyal to one and another.
Dyllan Holby, Grade 4

I believe in honesty because it's loyalty. God sent us down so we can be honest. It's a real good thing to do. To me, honesty means not lying to others or to adults. God made honesty for a good reason, so nobody in the world should lie.
Justin Bridges, Grade 4

Helpful
Obey
Nice
Equality
Sweet
Truth
Young
'Amber Jacobs, Grade 6

I believe in honesty because it means being nice. Sometimes I am not honest. But when I am honest, I feel glad because I'm not getting someone else in trouble. Honesty sometimes makes you get more friends.
Kyle Craighead, Grade 4

I believe in honesty because you tell the truth and don't lie. Tell the truth no matter what, even if you know you will get in trouble.
Shelby Harper, Grade 4

I believe in honesty because it never lies.
Mollie Prindiville, Grade 4

I believe in honesty because I think it is the right thing to do. It can help people to trust you and believe in you.
Bradley Morris, Grade 4

Honesty means to never tell lies. Honesty is telling the truth. Honesty means doing what you are supposed to do. Honesty is having courage to tell the truth even when it is not popular.
Ashley Reed, Grade 3

Don't tell a lie and don't look at someone else's paper. That's what honesty means.
Brandon Chambers, Grade 1

Being honest means that if a friend has something you want real bad, you don't take it.
Kayla Bush, Grade 1

You're honest if you always tell the truth and never tell a lie. Honest people never copy someone else's paper.
Abigail Garland, Grade 1

Honesty means to tell the truth and not to lie.
Landon Marek, Grade 4

If someone lies to the teacher and I know it, I will tell the teacher.
Billy Barr, Grade 2

Honorable
Obey
Nice
Earnest
Scruples
Truthful
You
Tazz White, Grade 6

    Once there was a boy. He was walking with his mom. There was a lady in front of them. She had a bag. The boy wondered what it was. She dropped it. It had money in it. She gathered up all the money. Then she set off again. The precise moment she dropped the bag, a car came by. The boy grabbed the money and thought of all the stuff he could buy. Then he saw the lady at a food stand. She said that she had no money and the man said she had to pay or go. The boy said, "Ma'am, you dropped this." She looked at the boy and gave him a hug. The boy felt better. The lady bought her food and went on.
Jeremy Sevier, Grade 6

    Honesty is telling the truth.
    Only you can make the decision to be honest.
    Knowing someone is being mean to someone else and not telling is not honest, so tell an adult you trust about it and don't be bullied because you made the right choice.
    Everyone is not honest all the time, but try to be honest as much as you can.
    Stand up for what you think is right; be honest about it, and don't stand and fight with fists because it will get you nowhere.
    Tell an adult you trust if someone is doing something wrong. If someone is beating someone else up, tell someone about it.
    You can make a world of difference just by being honest.
Thomas Howard, Grade 6

Honesty
Truthful, respectful
Hoping, caring, loving
Friends, neighbors, people, parents
Believing, trusting, willing
Believable, trustworthy
Becky
Sarah Cooper, Grade 7

I'm sorry I never told you the truth,
About that time when it would've been
Just me and you.
When I told you the answer to your question was "no,"
It was because I liked someone else,
And I didn't think you should've known.
I know I should have told you
About the person who was special to me,
But there was a problem, see?
He was your best friend.
I knew you cared about me
And maybe that's why.
Still, I had no right
To tell you a lie.
Lauren McCarty, Grade 8

Honesty
Nice, truthful
Working, talking, feeling
Truth, life, work, trust
Judging, making, telling
Frank, upright
Open
Devin Loftis, Grade 7

We think honesty is important for the whole world because otherwise people would steal and lie all the time. Recently, our nation was attacked by terrorists. Many honest people helped clean up the city and started helping others they didn't know. In the U.S. we also have Nobel Prize winners that tell the truth. A good example of honesty would be "Honest Abe" because he always told the truth. One time Abe got too much change for a book, and he walked about three miles to give it back.
Hardie Sorrels and Dillon Bane, Grade 4

Honorable
Obedient
Noble
Earnest
Saint
Truthful
Yielding
Drew Hulse, Grade 6

Honesty is not to tell a lie and to always tell the truth. If somebody asks you something, you should tell the truth. Even if your life is threatened, always tell the truth. We believe if you tell the truth, you will have a happy life.
Jimmy Bowers and Logan Bryan, Grade 4

I think honesty is telling the truth even if you're going to get in trouble. I think honesty is telling the truth.
Mark Sandoval, Grade 2

I think honesty is telling the truth and doing what you're told to do.
Greg Hulse, Grade 2

I think honesty is giving your heart to Jesus and being a Christian. To be Christian, you must talk to your preacher at church, then the preacher ducks your head in the water to baptize you.
Philip King, Grade 2

Honesty
Mrs. Lisa Stanley's Kindergarten Class

Honesty means being treated good.
Christina Anderson, Age 5

Honesty means being friendly and liking my sister.
Allison Dowell, Age 6

Honesty means not being silly.
Monya Nikahd, Age 5

Honesty means being nice, being friends and playing right.
Shelby Gullion, Age 5

Honesty means being good and kind.
John Shelton, Age 5

The Virtue of **Responsibility**

If I had a dog, I would be responsible for its well being. I'd feed it, love it and give it shelter. If had to, I would make sure it had the shots it needed. These responsibilities are worth the effort of having a dog!
Ryan Hackett, Grade 5

There was once a very irresponsible boy. His name was Jack. Jack never remembered anything he was supposed to do. He always forgot his book bag, and his poor mom always had to bring it to him. One day she would have no more of this. She said, "It's your responsibility to remember your book bag, young man." But Jack didn't listen. He again forgot his book bag and got in trouble. When Jack came home, his mother was waiting for him. The first words out of her mouth were, "You're grounded." Jack hung his head. "I know," he said. "I hope you've learned your lesson," she said sternly. "I have," Jack said slowly. And that's how Jack learned about responsibility.
Conner Garcia, Grade 3

My friend stole my eraser. I found out that somebody stole my eraser. I told him to tell me if he sees my eraser. And now I see him with my eraser. I told him never to steal again.
Josh Garcia, Grade 2

Once upon a time there was a twelve-year-old boy named Scott and his nine-year-old sister named Mary. They lived in the town of Lakeview and here's their story.

One day, Scott and Mary were making a lot of noise. "What's going on in there?" yelled their dad. "Nothing," they both said. "Yeah, right," said dad. "I'm watching football. Can you guys be quiet?" "Yes, sir," they both said. "I'll take a rest," said Mary. "I'll go play with Walline."

"Bark, bark, bark," said Walline, the dog. "Hey, Walline, what's up?" "Bark, grrr," growled Walline. "What? There's something in the basement?" asked Mary. "Grrr, bark!" replied Walline. "Okay, I'll go see. Look! Nothing." Walline kept growling. "What's that? Ahhh! Run inside! Dad, something's in the basement." "You were in the basement? Did you lock it back up?" asked dad. "I saw something with big black eyes, and it was hairy." "It was probably a raccoon or something," said dad. "You mean a mutated raccoon! It looked like this," said Mary, imitating the raccoon. "It did?" asked dad. "Well, I need to tell you something. I hoped you wouldn't find out, but when your mother and I moved into our new house, we kept a pet rabbit. One day we put the rabbit in the basement because it tried to eat one of your mother's hats. We forgot it overnight because of your baby shower. The next day we remembered it, so I went outside and opened the door. When I saw it, it scared me to death. So that's why there's a lock on the basement door, " explained dad. "Ok, I won't open it, " the children said.

The next day, Scott said, "Come on Mary, let's go outside and look at the mutated rabbit." When they got to the basement door, Scott changed his mind and said, "No Mary, don't open it, don't open it!" When Mary opened the door, Walline started to rush in. "No, Walline, don't go in! Close it, Mary, close the door!" "What's going on out there!" they heard dad say. "Dad, the thing ate the dog! Now instead of the dog eating the homework, the mutated rabbit ate the dog! Wait till my teacher hears about this!" said Mary. "I thought I told you both to stay out of the basement," dad said. "You're both grounded! Thanks for telling the truth, son."

Russell Lewis, Grade 5

Illustration by Cynthia Frick

I thank that responsibility is when your mom or dad tells you to clean up your toys.
Brock Fanchier, Grade 2

It is my responsibility to keep up with my friend's key chain, his book and his movie.
Matthew Barker, Grade 2

Responsibility is taking care of things. I have to keep my room clean.
Austin Hackett, Grade 1

I am responsible for taking care of my stuff. I have to put my bike by the garbage can.
Taia Ashworth, Grade 1

Your responsibility is to take care of something. I'm responsible for doing my homework.
Joy Lewis, Grade 1

Responsibility means feeding the dog.
Latasha Davis, Grade 1

I am responsible for doing my homework, putting it in my folder and bringing it back to school.
Ian Isbell, Grade 1

Responsibility means keeping up with stuff, like pencils and things.
Johnathan Dodd, Grade 1

Taking care of your stuff and cleaning your room every day is responsibility.
Andy Stamps, Grade 1

Responsibility is when you clean up your room, or when you mess it up, and no one helps you.
Austin Bryan, Grade 1

Responsibility is when I clean up my room, pick up my clothes and make my bed.
Jameson Sorrels, Grade 1

Responsibility means doing something you're supposed to do.
Drake Barr, Grade 1

Being respectful means you treat other people the way you want to be treated. You're always nice and treat everyone good.
J. T. Streng, Grade 1

Respect means that you should be very good and be responsible.
Brandi Shrum, Grade 2

Responsibility is always doing your best and doing what you are supposed to do. Being responsible is doing your schoolwork when your teacher tells you to or cleaning your room when your mom tells you to.
Andy Stamps, Grade 1

This is how to show responsibility. If you borrow something from someone, you need to give it back. If I say, "Can I use a piece of paper?" I give you a piece of paper back.
Emily Brown, Grade 2

If you are responsible you always do what you're supposed to do. When you tell someone you are going to do something, you do it.
Logan Watson, Grade 1

Responsibility
Accountable, liable
Trying, working, completing
Trust, faith, honesty, loyal
Laboring, toiling, accomplishing
Dependable, reliable
Believe
Blake Carter, Grade 8

We believe it is important to be responsible. You need to take care of your dirt bike or it will rust. If we don't take care of our relatives, they could get hurt or lost. Our animals would die if we didn't feed or water them. Laws must be followed or you will go to jail.
Kyle Bruce and Cole Condra, Grade 4

We believe in responsibility because if people were not responsible, things would not be done correctly or completely. When you are hurt and a reasonable person is not in charge, think what a bad situation could occur. Being prepared for school is a good responsibility. Taking care of yourself will give you a healthy life.
Ashley Buck and Chris Rodgers, Grade 4

We think that responsibility is doing what somebody expects you to do without being asked. If no one took responsibility, we wouldn't have anyone at school and their teachers would not come either. Responsible people run our jobs. For example, if the firemen were not responsible for putting out fires at buildings, they would burn. We all are responsible to do our job to make this world a better place to live.
Rachel Sandoval and Kasey Wright, Grade 4

We think it is very important to be responsible. We believe in responsibility because you should take care of situations yourself. If you made a promise, you should keep it. If you do not believe in responsibility and don't feed your pet, it will die. Being a responsible person will help us to succeed.
Cynthia Frick and Paige Robinson, Grade 4

We believe responsibility is right. One day a mom was going on a trip, but she could not find a babysitter. One child said they would stay with the other child. She was happy for their help, but said they must be responsible. When she went out the door, she said "Bye." Upon her arrival home, she was happy because everybody was all right and the child in charge was responsible.
Broderick Enoch and Alex Babbitt, Grade 4

I think responsibility means that if you had a pet, you would have to feed it and never stop feeding it. You would have to feed it every day and play with it a little every day.
Taylor Walker, Grade 2

I think responsibility means that if you got a pet animal, you should take care of it. If you don't take good care of your pet, it will die.
Michael Dobson, Grade 2

I think responsibility means picking up after yourself. I am cleaning up after myself.
Kristin Cook, Grade 2

I think responsibility is taking care of my dog and my cat. It also means taking care of the horse and the goats and the hogs and the cows.
Daniel Stewart, Grade 2

I think that responsibility is keeping up with your stuff. I also think that responsibility is not yelling out when somebody is looking.
Kaleb Woodcock, Grade 2

Responsibility means cleaning up and bringing home your books. Also, you should take care of your things.
Shrader Doray, Grade 2

Responsibility means picking up after yourself and helping others with their work.
Ashley Baynes, Grade 2

I think responsibility means that when somebody lets you borrow something and they ask you to keep up with it, then you should. I think responsibility is listening to others when they are talking. I also think responsibility means that if someone dropped their pencil box, you should help them pick it up. I also think responsibility means cleaning up your room and cleaning up after yourself. I also think responsibility means being nice to others and sharing with others.
Madeline Jennings, Grade 2

I think that responsibility is keeping up with your stuff. I think that responsibility is not yelling out when somebody is talking.
Kaleb Woodcock, Grade 2

Responsibility means to me caring for my books and getting to the school on time. Responsibility is doing my job—vacuuming.
Rebecca Fiehweg, Grade 2

I think that responsibility is cleaning my room up, taking care of my brother, keeping my desk clean at school, feeding my puppy at home, taking care of my horse and my cat, and keeping my house clean.
Justice McFall, Grade 2

If my mom says to clean my room, I will do it. I will be responsible to pick up my toys when my mom tells me to. If my teacher says to stop talking, I will do it. If she says to pull a card, I will do it. If my friend falls, I will go help her. I will go to the teacher and tell her I will be nice to her. If my teacher says to go to the chair, I will do it for my teacher.
Becky Cox, Grade 2

I think that responsibility is always doing what your mom says. I think that responsibility is cleaning up your bedroom when your mom says to. I think that responsibility is always listening to your mom.
Allison Jones, Grade 2

I think responsibility is taking care of my cat, feeding her, watering her, keeping her healthy, keeping dogs away from her, and letting her get a lot of exercise.
Megan Dowell, Grade 2

Responsibility means to take care of something that is not yours like a doll that is not yours that you took home and took care of.
Taylor Ford, Grade 2

Responsibility
Mrs. Judy Nosal's Kindergarten Class

Responsibility means you take care of yourself.
Amber Cooper, Age 5

Responsibility means you do something and you pick it up, not somebody else.
Kristen Dillon, Age 5

Responsibility means going outside and letting my dog use the bathroom.
Bobby Fraley, Age 6

Responsibility
Mrs. Lisa Stanley's Kindergarten Class

Responsibility means doing something right.
Kyle Fleming, Age 5

Responsibility means taking care of moms, dads, brothers and sisters.
Zane Horstmeyer, Age 5

Responsibility means telling people what to do.
Hailey Justice, Age 5

Responsibility means showing respect to friends.
Buddy Rollins, Age 5

Responsibility means playing with toys.
Chase Goolsby, Age 5

The Virtue of **Compassion**

Caring people play an active role in life.
Offering time to those in need is a key part of compassion.
Missions take in the cold and hungry people who don't have a home.
Pity is something you feel when you have compassion.
Accepting people is a large part of compassion.
Sympathy swept over our country the day the terrorists attacked.
Some Americans are sincerely sensitive to the needs of others.
Intensely mentally depressed people are people I have compassion for.
Our compassion outlasts that of people of other countries.
Needs are met by our countrymen as they rush to supply things for those in need.

 Someone who has compassion has a very caring soul and has a deep feeling for others. A compassionate person is one that has heartfelt honesty and mercy for others.
Ashley Lyles, Grade 6

Compassion is what I feel for you.
The way you talk and the things you do.
It's like the sunshine so bright and so new,
As blue as the sky as the day is new.
It's like the weeping willow with branches of sorrow.
I have compassion for you like there's no tomorrow
With tears that flow as a raging storm
And ends with a sound that's soft as a newborn.
Compassion, my friend, is what I have for you.
Ana Gregory, Grade 8

The day I found out he wasn't coming back,
I had convinced myself that everything was right on track.
He left his family; he left many friends.
He left his life with unfinished trends.
I keep pulling forward every hour of every day,
But every time I don't see him, it pulls me further away.
As I started getting over his death in my mind,
I found out someone else had left me behind.
I loved him so dearly; he was my best friend,
But he, too, had left unfinished trends.
It will be hard getting over those days.
Life will be like a big, giant maze.
They're still in my heart; their spirit will live on.
I hope that it's like they've never been gone.
We will keep living on until the very last.
But we will never forget our goods friends from the past.

In loving memory of Mike Baker and Bud Hoffman
A.J. Snider, Grade 8

There are so many ways that you can feel compassion for another person. A person who is compassionate will be with you to the bitter end. If you are compassionate then you show sympathy, have empathy, and most of all are just caring.

When you have sympathy, you are capable of feeling bad for someone. You are always feeling someone else's pain. You are able to listen and be a good friend. One time I showed sympathy when people were making fun of my brother, and no one understood but me.

A compassionate person has empathy. If someone is upset, it feels better if someone else has experienced it, too. They always know exactly how you feel. I've had empathy before when someone has lost a loved one or something like a pet.

If you have compassion then you are always caring about others' feelings. I would rather be with a caring person than anyone else. They are always great listeners and good comforters. I always try to be caring because I don't like to hurt people's feelings.

There are just so many ways that you can show compassion. Compassionate people will always show sympathy, have empathy and be caring to everyone.

Brittney Goode, Grade 7

When I look at the sunset,
My heart turns to stone.
I think of hurt people
And how people are alone.
I think of wars and battles
That gallant men have fought,
And that they were once kids
That other teachers taught.
Then I come to reality
And think it's all over,
When it's actual sorrow
That people really suffer.
Seth Barber, Grade 8

2 cups of love
1 cup of kindness
1/2 cup of care
1 tablespoon of friendship
1 teaspoon of loyalty

Mix together to create compassion.
Kathye Stone, Grade 6

The Virtue of **Loyalty**

L is for the love I had.
O is for how often we counted on each other.
Y is for you, my best friend.
A is for how awesome you are.
L is for your life.
T is for the trouble I had leaving you.
Y is for how young you were when you left me.
Jack Whetnall, Grade 8

Illustration by Patrick

FLAG

Faith in our country
Liberty for all
Allegiance to the United States
God and Country
Hunter Hudson, Grade 3

When I think of courage, I think of someone who is dependable. My friend Tatom is faithful. He is reputable, too.
Devin Jones, Grade 5

When you are loyal, you are faithful and dependable.
I am very loyal when I am dependable, like when my sister needs me or when my Aunt Teresa needs help with cleaning.
Chelsea Odom, Grade 5

Loyalty means friendship.
You use it every day.
When you go to the movies,
You offer to pay his way.
When asked to keep a secret,
Loyalty is a must.
When your friend tells you something,
You keep your big mouth shut.
Josh Bryan, Grade 6

If you have loyal friends, you have trust. If you have a loyal family, you have faith. If you have loyal teachers, you have people who care for you. You can experience the good things about loyalty.
LaJerrica Cowan, Grade 6

Loyalty is believing in something
And fighting for something you love.
When you fight for something,
It's a gift from above.

People in the Army
Are very loyal to us.
They fight for our country,
Others make no fuss.

Policemen are very loyal,
They keep us out of dangers.
They will always protect us
From hurtful men and strangers.

Firemen are also loyal,
They help us every day.
They always have a chance to hurt us,
But they throw that chance away.

Now that we know what loyalty is,
We can all be loyal.
We can fight for something we love.
We would be using the gift from above.
Tabitha Dailey, Grade 6

Loyalty is standing behind someone in good times or bad. Loyalty is being there for them whether they are happy or sad. We should be loyal and true to our country, especially to the old red, white and blue.

A loyal friend will be there to the end. So if they have faith in you, you have faith in them.
Will Hightower, Grade 6

Loyalty
Rich or fame
No matter what you do,
You should always be treated the same.
Giving loyalty is a way to find friendship, not shame
In each day and every other way.
Calvin Starks, Grade 7

Loyalty means I will have to be faithful to you.
I'll trust you if you can trust me.
Friendship is a part of loyalty.
Loyalty means I have to have faith and so do you!
I'll help you through good times and bad.
We'll be the best of friends if we are loyal to each other.
Jennifer Hollis, Grade 6

Loyalty is friendship
It has the relationship
That you are true
And you're there for them.

Friendship is caring
And could mean sharing.
You're fair if you care.

Friendship means
You're close friends
And also means
You're nice.

If you're friends,
You will always
Be there for them.

So this is what
Friendship means,
Which has a
Relationship
With loyalty.
Maggie Thompson, Grade 6

When you are loyal
Then you have friends who trust you.
Loyalty means love
That came from above.

Loyal friends love you,
And you love your friends, too.
They would care for you always.
They will think you are true.
Amber Carney, Grade 6

Are you loyal?
Are your friends loyal to you?
Loyalty is the biggest part of friendship.
Will you stick by your friends through thick and thin
No matter what situation they are in?
Not only under one condition,
Be loyal til the end.
Asia Clark, Grade 8

What does it mean to be loyal?
Loyalty means to be true
And to help others when they are blue.

Loyalty is to love and to cherish,
Like a loved one sweet as a dove
Until it shall perish.

Hopefully this answered your questions.
If you have a loved one that you want to be loyal,
Then ask questions.
I'm sure they would be open for suggestions.
Chad Fisher, Grade 8

I have a virtue I'd like to share.
It won't take long, so don't pull your hair.
I'm talking about loyalty; it's very rare.
I'll begin right now—it started with care.

That means stick with your friends through thick and thin.
Making them happy just takes a grin.
Stand by your friend no matter what.
To have a friend you have takes a thought.
Jeremy Officer, Grade 8

Are yours friends loyal to you?
Are your friends truthful?
Do they stick by you?
Are they with you all the time?
Do you take every minute with them for granted?
Are you happy that they're alive?
Are they with you through the good times?
Do they enjoy them with you?
Do they stick with you through the hard times?
Do they endure them as you do?
You have just taken the test.
Did you answer yes?
Brittany Pickler, Grade 8

As I sit and wonder about the people who are loyal,
As I sit and wonder about the people who care,
As I sit and wonder about the people who are fair,
I sit and I think that I should have to wonder at all
Because my friends are loyal
And I can count on them all.
Lorie Diane Marsh, Grade 8

The earth is deep with a soul,
Everything inside it makes it whole.
It contains many different creatures,
Along with many beautiful features.
Even though it is full of sin,
The Lord keeps loving it from deep within.
From Him, we should all learn a lesson.
Rebekah Marie Wolfenbarger, Grade 8

This story is going to be about a couple that is loyal, so sit back and listen to what I have to say about their life. The girl's name is Ashley. She is fourteen and in high school. The boy's name is Michael; he is fifteen and also in high school. They have a lot of classes together and make good grades. Ashley is on the basketball team and Michael is on the track team. They both are loyal to their friends and to their school. They are both in F.C.A. Ashley wants to play for Pat Summit when she gets older. Michael wants to be a scientist.

A year later, Ashley turned fifteen and a month later Michael turned seventeen. Michael would help Ashley with her homework, and then one day Michael said that he didn't want to help her anymore. They broke up. Michael was so sad that he would not talk to anyone. Their friends tried to get them back together, but they both said that they had better things to do than go out. They also were not loyal to their friends. They told them that they didn't like them, even though they did.

Then one day, Michael went up to Ashley and said, "I still have feelings for you." Ashley said, "I have feelings for you, too." Then they got back together, and one day Michael asked Ashley to marry. Ashley said "Yes!" Five years later they had kids, and they were loyal all the time. They named their girls Tara and Brandi and their boy Anthony.

They had to get a bigger house so all of them could have their own rooms. Then one day Michael and Ashley went to a party, and when they were coming home, a big truck hit them head on. Everybody that knew them all said that they were the most loyal people they had ever known. They were so good to their family and friends. Ashley never got to live her dream. So her sister did it for her.

The kids had to go live at one of their aunt's house. The youngest child, Tara, never really knew her mom and dad. She got to know them by what people told her about them. When they got older they went to their parents' graves every day. Then one day Anthony went into the military. He said he was doing this because his father would want him to. He came back one day, and the first thing he did was go to the grave and see how his mom and dad were doing. The first thing he said was, "I miss y'all." Then he started telling them what he had done for four years. He got married and had kids. They all lived a nice life.

Ashley Cook, Grade 7

Loyalty is feeling,
But very revealing.
Loyalty is the best,
So put it to the test!
Be fair,
But don't forget to share.
Have trust in another,
Just don't burst out all your personal secrets.
Go find new friends,
But remember to be kind.
Loyalty is faith.
To have faith,
To believe in another
Is all the loyalty you will ever need!
Shara Garcia, Grade 7

    Loyalty means different things to various people. I am going to tell you a story about how one girl finds it in her heart to be loyal and stand up for what she believes in. I hope that this story will help you be able to stand up for what you believe in.

    Mari is devoted to her religion. Her best friend, Anna, respects Mari for herself. One day at school a boy named Bob saw them talking. They were talking about Mari's believing in fears.

    Bob told Billy, his best friend, about what he heard. Soon, afterwards, they started to make fun of Mari. When Polly heard this, she told Miss Kagon, their teacher.

    The next day Miss Kagon taught the class that it is okay to stand up for what they believe in.
J.J. Fannin, Grade 7

Be loyal to me; I'll be loyal to you.
Loyalty comes from the inside and
It leaks through!

Trust is all about loyalty.
You trust me and
I'll trust you.

Loyalty is telling someone something
And the person should not be a rat.
So trust someone, and that's that!

Loyalty is being able to trust someone.
You tell me a secret, I keep it a secret.
Loyalty is being there when someone needs a friend.
Friends trust, friends care.
If you have loyalty in a friend, they're always there.
Amber Mizelle, Grade 7

                    Loyalty
               True, trustworthy
          Believing, trusting, caring
        Friends, family, school, church
       Community, city, town, county
         Loving, sharing, responding
            Devoted, obedient
                      Me
Patrick Hall, Grade 8

Hello, my name is Tara McClenon, and I'm going to tell you a story about a boy named Pete. You might be able to relate to some of the characteristics in this story. Pete is even going to go through some things he's never been through before. So sit back and relax and enjoy.

One day a boy named Pete had just woken up from a long dream. He got up and got ready for his first day at high school. He put on his clothes and shoes. He was ready to go. He put on his cologne and combed his hair; he made it real slick and shiny. He started out the back door.

He walked up the street when he saw a strange boy coming towards him. He looked very hard to make sure it wasn't someone he knew. It wasn't. Then he thought for a minute, he's a new person in town, I should go introduce myself.

He ran over to the boy and said, "Hi, my name is Pete Anderson, but they call be Pete." The boy was amazed. "Hi, my name is David Martin." "Is this your first day of school at high school?" "Yes," said David. "Me, too." "So where did you move here from?" "Atlanta, Georgia." Pete didn't know where that was so he just went on walking.

They finally arrived at high school. When they walked in the school, they were amazed by all the people who were there. There were tall, short, and medium-sized students. When they arrived at their new classrooms; they were excited. They saw all types of things, like pictures, birds and other things.

Well, the day got started, and everybody was quiet when the teacher came in. This teacher looked mean and vicious. It was a man teacher; his name was Thomas Allen. He pointed to the board saying, "My name is Thomas Allen. I will be your first period teacher for English every day. Here are your schedules."

He got started on the lesson. It was on editing sentences. As the day went on, it got stranger. It was like everybody was going crazy. Finally it was time to go home.

Pete waited on David to come out of the school when all of a sudden, he saw him getting beat up by some students. Pete went over and tried to stop them. When he came, they ran. "Are you okay?" Pete asked. No answer. He tapped David on the shoulder. "Are you okay?" "Yeah," said David. "I'll be all right." Pete picked him up and they went on walking back to their houses.

Almost a week had passed and David was still getting beat up. Pete had to find a way to stop this. He thought and thought. "I've got it! I'll teach him how to take up for himself." After school he told David the idea and David said he would agree to it.

Every day after school, he taught David how to take up for himself. He taught him how to walk away and ignore bullies. After a couple of weeks, David started to get the hang of it. It took him over two months to learn.

When it came time to go to school the next day, David got scared. He went through all his classes thinking about what was going to happen at the end of the day. It got so bad that he could not even concentrate. He was in his last class when the bell rang. He went to his locker, gathered his things and walked outside.

When he walked outside, the bullies started to surround him. He said, "Please leave me alone. I haven't done anything to you." They still didn't let him go. They beat him up again and Pete had to help him. Pete said, "Why didn't you do what I told you to do?" "I did," David replied, "but they still beat me up again today." Pete thought and thought until he could not think anymore.

Friday came, and Pete just had to find away to help David. That whole weekend he thought about it. On Saturday he thought of a plan. Maybe David hadn't been aggressive enough when he told the bullies to leave him alone. Yeah! Pete was determined that David could do it this time.

When they went back to school on Monday, Pete told David what his plan was, and David agreed. David went through all his classes very nervous. He was shaking and moving as he walked down the hallway. David was so scared he skipped lunch.

Finally, the end of the day came. David was back where he started. The clock struck three o'clock and the bell rang. He went to his locker, packed his things and got ready to leave.

There was Pete ready for him to come and face the bullies. Pete had so much faith in David; he knew he could stand up to them. He walked out of the school very slowly. He heard Pete saying, "You can do it, all you have to do is believe." David went up to the bullies and said, "Leave me alone. I haven't done anything to you so stop!" When they heard this they left.

"You did it! You did it!" said Pete. "I knew you could." From that day on, the bullies never messed with David again. Pete knew David could do it; he had a lot of loyalty toward David.

I've just told you a story about two boys named David and Pete. Pete went through a whole lot of thinking. He went through some things he'd never been through before, and David got beat up every day because he was new in town and he was a geek. The moral of this story is this: Never give up hope and always be loyal to your friends. Always be there for them.

I hope you enjoyed this story. Don't forget to be loyal to everybody you know.
Tara McClenon, Grade 7

                Loyalty
           Faithful, honest
     Benefiting, caring, trusting
        Faith, love, joy, hope
    Longing, enduring, forgiving
         True, everlasting
            Trustworthy
Kristina Johnson, Grade 8

When I hear the word loyalty,
I do what my heart tells me to do.

When I hear the word loyalty,
I know I should love, be honest,
And have respect for you.

So when you hear the word loyalty,
I think these are some of the things
You should do.
Lorenzo Sawyers, Grade 8

The word loyalty
is special to the
heart.
It means
that friends
will never part.
Even though
they have fights,

they make
it work,
They sleep
good at night
knowing
they have
friends that
are loyal.
Kimberly Bendt, Grade 8

I once told a friend a secret and told her not to say.
She said, "I will not on a majestic mountain or on a beautiful shiny
   bay."

People begged her to say, but she knew I would move away.
She said she could not say, not even on a shiny bay.

I said to her, "That is loyalty, king of all royalty."
I am glad she is my friend and a friend she will stay.
Brittany Morrison, Grade 8

As my friend asked one thing,
I promised him I would not tell.
He told me something I would not sing,
He told me he had failed.
He did not succeed at what I tried.
I made a promise I said I would keep,
For if I did not I knew I would cry.
And as I lie about to sleep,
I know this promise I will forever keep.
No temptation will penetrate,
For my loyalty is great.
Tom Cruz, Grade 8

Loyalty is one who shows respect to all,
In every situation they make you feel tall.
Friends are very trustful in every way,
You can call on them any day.
Going out nightly and looking for families every day,
But not getting paid.
So they go, fight, and win, until the end.
Shada Carter, Grade 7

The people of New York are very caring
They let the people use their things, which means they're sharing.
If something happened to me, I would want them to be
Just as they were to the people on the scene.
Leah Morgan, Grade 7

They had loyalty in their eye,
As they looked into the sky.
As the men watched the plane,
They all thought how insane.
They went into the building to fight,
And through the fight, they saw the light,
And knew it would be all right.
Dana Sorrells, Grade 7

Loyalty
Truthful, caring
Comply, daring, follow
Friend, love, devotion, obedience
Submit, serve, obey
Respectful, dutiful
Observance
Sarah Alsup, Grade 7

Loyalty is what everybody needs. Loyalty means caring, silliness and having feelings for people.

The first part of loyalty is caring for people. You need to be caring to your family and your friends. They might need you for a helping hand one day.

The next thing is silliness. You can always be silly to friends because it can make them feel good.

Finally, you need to have feelings. I think you need to have feelings because if you laugh at your friends, then they will laugh at your when you are sad.

These are the things you need to be loyal: caring, silliness and feelings.

Shawna Shrum, Grade 8

The angels in the starry sky looked down on the little boy. They said he had a special gift that no one could take away.

"What?" the boy asked.

All at the same time, the angels answered, "Loyalty."

They quickly explained loyalty meant having faithfulness for someone or something.

The little boy was disappointed because it didn't sound like much at all. They told him that loyalty was a wonderful thing to have, and if he was loyal to them, the loyalty would be returned.

Crystal Tucker, Grade 7

The Virtue of **Work**

Work
Willingly
Officially
Respectfully
Kindly
Garrett Fanchier, Grade 6

Work
Tired, fun
Running, folding, ironing
Clothes, iron, dishes, carpet
Cooking, washing, vacuuming
Hot, busy
Labor
Andrica Leach, Grade 6

Work
Hard, fun
Running, working, hammering
Hammer, level, square, wood
Drilling, painting, mudding
Hot, cold
Workers
Joseph Wilson, Grade 6

Work
Want, tired
Driving, running, grinding
Boy, woman, man, girl
Working, painting, hammering
Hot, cold
Lightning
Casey Boyd, Grade 6

Hard, stressful
Folding, drying, washing
Clothes, shoes, socks, jewelry
Talking, sleeping, cleaning
Loud, hard
Housewife
Jessica Etheridge, Grade 7

Work
Hard, easy
Building, running, grabbing
Wood, hammer, nails, screwdriver
Painting, cutting, drilling
Hard, fast
Improvement
Terrence Coggins, Grade 7

Work
Heavy, large
Dumping, pulling, hauling
Loader, crane, dozer, grader
Driving, controlling, moving
Equipment
Josh Dickson, Grade 8

Work
Farming, ranching
Pulling, plowing, growing
Corn, tobacco, wheat, cotton
Eating, chewing, picking
Sweet, soft
Life
Brian Sevier, Grade 8

Printed in the United States
4157